EMBRACING FEMININE ENERGY

EMBRACING FEMININE ENERGY

SERAPHINA WILDE

CONTENTS

CHAPTER 1

Introduction to Feminine Energy

Feminine energy and women have gone through a deeply intense transformational journey. In the process, men and the masculine are also transformed. This book is devoted to revealing the depth and hope of embracing feminine qualities. This book follows parts 1 and 2 of this series which discuss the influence of the feminine, self-care, dating, and embodying unconditional love, particularly in the most intimate circle of our lives.

Delving into the world of love, particularly the conservative nature of faith and passion that walks alongside it, naturally encompasses tapping into the feminine. Love itself is a source of nourishment. It must, therefore, be embraced by two nurturing entities: a state or the people who embody it. It isn't just an emotional embrace that we go through in this particular state of existence. And it isn't something that is done to us or for us. It is something that we, the people involved, take part in. It is a willingness to challenge expectations and to revolt against loneliness and frustration. Making use of our receptive energy, we have the means to transform not just ourselves but the entire collective, for the bonds of love that we devise are far-reaching and long-lasting. It isn't just a physical transformation. It's an energetic field that is collectively charged by us, drawing in those beings that are desperate to share in care and symbols of passion erected by an entire population, for an entire population.

Defining Feminine Energy

Feminine energy can be described as the life force behind women and the internal anchor of a man's reactivity in the world. It activates and emphasizes female experiences and abilities, from help and encouragement to inspiration and sexual love. It is also the operative standard for how commercial and career assertions interact with a female physiology. The energy of the feminine can be conveyed and lived at different times through different cultures and experiences, but there is not one type of personality or experience that is "really" the feminine.

In terms of gender, qualities and strengths associated with feminine energy include emotional awareness, empathy and compassion, surrender and openness. This does not make women superior in these characteristics in comparison to men, nor does it suggest that men are weak or damaged by identifying with these values. Sensitivity indicates openness to emotions as well as heightened sensory, intellectual, and interpersonal abilities. A developed sensitivity enhances one's intuitive intelligence and deepens the potential for meaningful relationships. Devotion carries deep feeling; men and women are equally alive in this quality, oriented towards service, towards giving. Passive receptivity accompanies active giving. Annunciatory intelligence means reading each moment and taking the action that corresponds with the spiritual potential contained therein. Devotion drives these actions, helping you to "see Christ," to recognize the living essence in every other creature.

CHAPTER 2

Understanding Masculine and Feminine Dynamics

The battlefield of love and relationships is influenced and, in most cases, dominated by the dynamics between men and women. This can be summed up as the psychology between masculine and feminine energy. So, it is worth understanding the energies and their playing patterns as both these energies work on a universal law. Energy is something which is beyond the physical world and is the most basic form of all matter and engulfs the whole universe. To make it easier and known concepts, feminine energy can be understood as yin, and the masculine can be related to yang.

To have more practical value, one can understand that yin is pure void - the physical part, and yang is the kinetic part - the process part. Every material is composed of void and particles. As of now, it will be more clear that men represent physical reality and women symbolize kinetic or process reality. Feminine energy is the empty and void part, so it can be filled in, and masculine part is the one which fills in the void of feminine for creation. When creation occurs, the void part again becomes empty for another process. So the basic idea of yin supports it as all that takes place (yang) transpires within the void. So the void part envelops all within it - it embraces, engulfs, contains, and magnetizes everything. Feminine energy is very mesmerizing and inviting, which acts as a cohesive force, gravitational force, and draws everything towards itself, inspiring and influencing. So, the feminine energy is so powerful that it has the cumulative effect to attract, and even if the opposing part reacts negatively or tries to suppress a feminine part, it will ultimately be drawn by its influence. All the apparent hardness or repulsion of the object will have a hidden bond between it.

Exploring Traditional Gender Roles

Women have been oppressed in society for a very long time. That is old news. I've realized, though, that we've been oppressing men as well, in a way which is less talked about. And we've been doing it through denying our own softer, more feeling energies which can draw them to us. According to traditional gender roles, men are fixers and women are feelers. When the woman feels bad she should talk and talk about it, and the man listens and tries to fix the situation by giving advice. But we can't cleave gender roles anymore. They belong to a "stage" in the evolution of humanity that has ended. This is why the traditional "man" approach can't relate romantically to many modern "woman" approaches. We must change. This has shown itself in my own dating life.

Today, sensuality and emotionality are considered feminine, while the man is expected to provide intellectual stimulation and sexual direction. Unfortunately, talk is cheap. A woman who thinks she is getting a sensitive man is ideally getting a primitive man because a sensitive woman is what really evokes male emotion. She may be in for a rude awakening. Let's allow ourselves to become more emotionally volatile to light our men up sexually. It sounds childish to us because the expressive, bigger the emotional more on society has given to women. Men don't have that same luxury. Necessary, we tend to suppress these emotions because men are traditionally assumed to be rational, calm figures in crises. We have been taught to take charge and to do things logically. Perfection and efficiency are our cults.

CHAPTER 3

The Power of Vulnerability in Men

The mark of a man who is comfortable in his masculine energy is that he fears nothing. Fearlessness, however, does not equate to heartlessness or gruffness. And one of the most underrated human emotions that masculine men must live with is vulnerability. Vulnerability from a man feels weak because he is often up against the lifelong habit of not allowing certain emotions to be okay.

It's important for a man to embrace his feminine energy. Not only will it make him an ideal romantic partner, but it will also make him a better human being. Vulnerability can be a very good thing; rather than displaying weakness, it can have quite a transformative effect. First, it dispels the stereotypical alpha-male characteristics. It might seem strange, even paradoxical, to think that sensitivity isn't a weakness, but it starts creating some real depth for the female brain. It shows her that you're not just the same as every other man – that you're deeper. When she sees you're not just the same alpha-male stereotype as everyone else, it's at this point that she really begins falling in love – because you're now a real human being to her.

Practicing vulnerability can spell loneliness for the man who isn't surrounded by sympathetic 'misunderstandings'. But men are often missing the real masculinity inside themselves, as well, because until they are comfortable with vulnerability they will always be playing a role, or a part, rather than acting out of their passion. Vulnerability transforms a woman's intense emotions from anger to attraction – the same goes for men.

Breaking Down Stereotypes

Stereotypically, men are not supposed to feel deeply, cry profusely, touch tenderly, or express vulnerability. We have created an image of men as stoic and strong, not swayed by emotion, tears, or soft, sensitive touches. This stereotype doesn't reflect who men truly are but has instead constricted human expression and feeling. Constricted men love, joy, passion, caring, nurturing, tenderness, openness, openness to love, vulnerability, softness, and empathy create a considering heart space that is extremely small, rigid, and often reactive. Men who want to experience passion, the joy of laughter over something silly, love, or openness need to strip off the layers that keep them confined into unrealistic manhood roles. Opening themselves to the considered feminine energy becomes their 3rd step in embracing their feminine energy.

If potential feminine energies are located within us, why is it that men refrain from embracing, honoring and loving themselves through the feminine? The reason stems from collectively held beliefs that surrounding vulnerability are wrong or portray weakness. With each reading there will be resistance that arises within some men, simply due to years of conditioning that has told them it is not okay to express their tears, their fears, or their uncertainties. The knees will jerk up, the voice within may start pummeling out defensive barbs, and the heart rate elevates. The quickest response to quiet this is to create a space within the whole system that will break down those elements of judgment, criticism, and trepidation. Gently and with Divine timing, the walls will crumble, and space will be permitted to understand, to feel the words, and become an embodiment of embracing energies that will serve.

CHAPTER 4

Cultivating Emotional Intelligence

The fourth quality you must cultivate to integrate feminine energy is emotional intelligence. More specifically, men must learn the importance of empathy, compassion, and emotional awareness. These are the cornerstones of emotional intelligence and are crucial to the building of successful connections.

Empathy and compassion are inextricably linked. You cannot exhibit one without the other. However, this doesn't mean the two are synonymous. Compassion is empathy in action, or putting oneself in the shoes of others and acting accordingly.

Traits displayed by someone who is emotionally intelligent include kindness and compassion while exhibiting a commitment to service or a sense of community. Being present is another trait, or giving one's undivided attention to someone else and being actively engaged in the moment.

Emotional intelligence-related traits also include agreeability, or working as part of a team and having strong interpersonal skills. Other traits include conscientiousness, which involves exhibiting a willingness to go the extra mile while showing strength in character.

Emotional intelligence also involves displaying emotional self-aware-ness, using strengths to meet goals, and earning the trust of others.

Finally, this type of intelligence also includes long-term visionary leadership, or having a desire to make a difference in society and showing a commitment to pastoral care or mentoring. Building re-lationships is a man's duty and responsibility. When that happens, something powerful is triggered in the man's psyche. He changes magically and inexplicably, simply through learning the value and the machinations of his feelings. The more connected he is to him-self and those around him, the better, more authentic, and sexual he will be. However, the most important point to be made about emo-tional intelligence is its ability to transform a man not just on the in-side but on the outside as well.

Empathy and Compassion
Empathy and compassion. When it comes to romantic relation-ships, it is generally accepted that a high degree of emotional intel-ligence is vitally important to their expected success. For McQueen and Waller (2009) and Wenkoff and Lewis (2008), this emotional intelligence has two components: empathy and compassion. Emo-tionally intelligent men are sympathetic or empathetic to the suf-fering of other men and, out of their empathy or sympathy, desire to bestow physical and emotional well-being upon them. Empathy is the identification with and understanding of another's situation, feelings, and motives. Baumeister and Bushman (2007) suggest that empathy is the precursor to compassion. If one can understand and appreciate the suffering of others through empathy, they are flipping the coin to a nurturing and compassionate response. Compassion is the positive and nurturing affect that arises out of this empathetic understanding of another's situation and moves one to give of self to lessen the perceived suffering of another. Taken together, empa-

thy and compassion make the person who is less 'suffering' or less 'healed' know that he is cared about by another, and the two will feel more connected as a result.

A woman's mind, inside and out, is an intricate labyrinth of feelings and emotions. And men need to have an empathetic and compassionate mind and tender touch to traverse it; they just need to be ready to slow down and follow her lead. Providing some emotion and care in the moment is likely to greatly increase your efficacy in a heart-to-heart conversation, especially in times of crisis. Although you might feel as though you're talking to a wall, subtle body language changes can show a marked difference in the softenings men notice over time. Want to know more ways to develop the care factor? Keep an eye out for any number of workshops on equality, domestic violence, respectful attitudes, and unhealthy relationship cessation and prevention. They are very likely to show you a thing or two about putting action to better use than words when it comes to care and consideration.

CHAPTER 5

Healing Past Trauma and Conditioning

What might be standing between you and truly embracing a woman, her deep femininity, and feminine essence, is trauma from past relationships or deep conditioning from being brought up in a world that teaches men that femininity is weak and that masculinity is the epitome of strength. This can be a difficult wound and conditioning to see, as it is wound within ourselves. How can we see a belief and behavior pattern in which we are deeply entrenched when it is so pervasive as to also be in our subconscious? It demands deep self-reflection, awareness, and a large amount of healing.

Healing can be viewed as cleaning off energetic gunk. As we start to heal past trauma from relationships, we open ourselves to embracing femininity in women. This offers most men the bonus of also opening themselves to women and communication—being able to be real, open, and vulnerable. We all get to learn a bit about how deep these past traumas or conditioning have hidden in our subconscious. The term healing has also been abused in its usage when it is related to feminine energy. For a man, especially, it can often be associated with being weak emotionally. We have been brought up in a world that harbors the philosophy that we are fine—emotionally, mentally, spiritually, and somatically—as long as we are 'hard.' We often equate healing to be somehow losing our emotional shell of hardness for some substitute—even love. The philosophy does hold true for when we are in the midst of healing. We often feel as if we have been stripped down to the bone, not understanding what has been done to us. It takes a strong man to understand the importance of healing and to invest in the process.

Self-Reflection and Awareness

Men can learn to become more present in the moment by becoming more aware of thought patterns, learned behavior, and social conditioning. They can begin to stop the behaviors and thoughts that are barriers to learning and practicing feminine energy. Most of us are quite aware of our behavior and the consequences, but most of the barriers stem from wanting to change but not knowing how in a collective chaotic world. As the people, clients, and collective society shift and change, we observe our potential to transform inside the new age we are already part of. This is a legitimate plea to look at ourselves and buy into individual and self-transformation.

To learn to embody feminine energy, the energy of love, men must have an understanding and a full awareness of who they are and the intelligence to question learned behaviors, thoughts, and potentials. Awareness is noticed and comes from within a human being as they experience their mind and heart. To be emotionally calm and accessible is to be aware. All humans are born with full awareness, and it is the damage and conditioning that steers away from heart intelligence. In our opinion, women are not the complex beings of heightened intuition, but as we are stripped of some of the burden and conditioning of our ego mind, we notice and heal to create a clearer and present life filled with love, kindness, and yearning potential.

CHAPTER 6

Embracing Sensitivity and Intuition

Another critical aspect of the feminine aspect is being able to be sensitive to what is happening and able to sense the energies - the emotions, thoughts, desires, intentions - of those around them. A lot of women may already be in touch with this part of themselves, since it is part of their feminine energy, but do not honor it. It might have been taught that men do not like clingy, emotional, or intuitive women. There is a beauty to being deep and taking the time to develop emotional intelligence and sensitivity, while encouraging the men in their lives to be open and share more deeply who they are and what is happening for them. Just as men need to be reprogrammed, so do women. Women need to trust that many men do want this, but may not be sure how to be open themselves.

Machismo has programmed men to repress and inhibit the feminine aspect of themselves that is intuitive and sensitive. It is often encouraged in men that the harder the man is the more stoic and senseless they are. But this is not really in a man's nature and is only a role that they are playing. Love and passion can only arise from a place of emotional depth and sensitivity. As long as we live in a state of mind-centered being, in a state of superficiality, we are not really living at all. I invite women to go to the depth, to go inwards, and really see, understand, and love the men in their lives. Not the mask, the pretense, the super-ego, the hidden fear and the artificiality, but their core, their essence, their being. Once the way is opened for deeper emotional connection, love and spark can be reignited. And, best of all, we do it in a way that still welcomes, honors and nurtures the foundational masculine presence.

Honoring Emotional Depth

Honoring emotional depth in a man, acknowledging that he just might be hurt or disappointed, or tired, will affect every dynamic of personal and relational experience. How can a man begin to bring forth his own depths of emotion when those around him won't even acknowledge they exist? For a moment, choose to throw out the belief systems that teach men should not cry or that male tears are signs of a show of weakness or, worse, an absence of masculinity. Forget statements that might remind us of our fathers, uncles, or coaches. And if you're a man reading this, forget that those tears of your own might have made you feel guilty, shamed, or less than a man. In acknowledging a man's emotional depth as an essential part of who he is, we embrace our femininity.

In other words, for a man to come home to his femininity, to love a woman with depth, passion, empathy, and emotional insight, those around him must be willing to not only see that depth when he comes but also to honor it as well. So how does a man learn to awaken to his potential for emotional depth, to welcome that depth into his life? Let's see. There will be those who will straight-out and unapologetically tell you that to be masculine means you must embrace a stoic posture of unyielding strength. But if experience teaches us more than theory ever could, then it would appear we have made an error. A man's tears do not weaken the impression of us; they reaffirm emotional connections with each other. And more importantly, they confirm our embrace of our own feminine fervor.

CHAPTER 7

Balancing Strength and Softness

In the context of embracing feminine energy, it is vital for those socialized as male to find the right balance between their strength and their softness. This is where a myth (that is not taken as science) comes up. It would be good to weave a new myth, a better story about not globbing more toxic masculinity on men. We are seeing in so many places the recipe for how men can't be and how masculinity should not exist. We are missing someone dreaming a co-creative story that brings hope to how both qualities can grow in all people, socially raised woman or man in body.

Both of the sexes need a healthy helping of finding safety and respect in blending the qualities typically identified as male with the qualities identified as female. If the goals of feminism are looked at on a continuum, the very edge of that movement up to the present, they can be said to revolve around protecting the rights of women and growing those collective rights. A wider, more relational way of looking at those rights that actually involves building infrastructure to foster the nurturing parts of our human potential is on the horizon. It is calling every single person to work on that infrastructure. It is clearly calling women towards leadership, and there too we must call on embracing a powerful blend of both energies.

The Myth of Toxic Masculinity

Despite the shifts in modern gender roles, there still exists a deeply entrenched myth of toxic masculinity. This insidious lie takes the positive virtues of courage and resilience and twists them into hammers to terrify boys and men into emotional suppression, violence, and even suicide. Women hear of toxic masculinity and they hear the language of domination, privilege, and oppression. Women hear the recovery movement's idea that the undoing of men's toxic socialization requires all of society to be 'safe', to love, to nurture, to 'support the sharing of oneself'.

We offer in place of this social psychological myth a new vision of what once was - and always is - a specialized and balanced form of 'men's love'. At all times, in all societies, there are particular roles, virtues, and loves which are specifically associated almost exclusively with men; men know that it is their duty as men to fulfill these loves. We do not claim that men are only or innately anything. We call these loves 'masculine' not because only men can have them but because women rarely do. We don't push the gender-neutral idea that men's nurturing, protective, and disciplinary loves are the same things as women's - rather, we argue that men's nurturing, protective, and disciplinary love are 'masculine' when men, because of who they are as men, express them in specifically masculine ways.

Above all else, masculine nurture empowers independence - giving strength and wisdom that enable the power of masculine virtues like resilience, courage, self-starting, and inventive power.

CHAPTER 8

Building Healthy Relationships

Upon abandoning masculinity defined by domination and embracing feminine energy, it is also of utmost importance to show love to the feminine essence without claiming to change the object of such love or expecting something in return automatically. It is significant to remember that the roots of many social issues can be found in poor communication. Also, communication is always a "two-way street," meaning it should convey deep emotions in both directions and require active listening.

In the topic at hand, "active listening" is advised as the best way to pay attention and understand, which can produce a strong emotional connection and intuition.

Communication is the key to building healthy relationships. In this chapter, the focus is on learning how to be a good listener and how to ask with care and good intentions. It is important to effectively communicate oneself, exposing feelings regardless of culture, rather than hiding them until they erupt. Active listening is an important step toward embracing feminine energy. It is important to allow feminine energy to take priority while in the mental state of hearing and trying to understand oneself. In this situation, a woman needs communication as a liquid form of understanding, not just a one-way exchange of secrets or information. Men need to have a strong commitment to active listening, tenderness, gentleness, and care, and this needs to be actively managed. Communication must be explicit, easily understood, without any superior or dominant undertones. It also requires an understanding of the "unique feminine feeling" and how to unlock it.

Communication and Active Listening

Communication, taking time to talk with each other 'heart to heart', is about finding intimacy. When we communicate from the heart, we lay the foundations for deep connection. There are basically two types of communication: we are either communicating a defense or an out-of-control emotion. Defense communication is based on preconceived beliefs and what we think we know about ourselves, our partner, and love in general.

When you are experiencing overpowering emotions, the message you send out tends to be 'Keep away, I need space'. However, this is not considered a healthy response to an emotional attack. It creates emotional distance. The message you really want to convey when you are upset is: 'Stay with me, listen and understand me'. This is not always an easy message to convey. It is vital for people in relationships together to understand that focusing on one issue at a time helps you stay focused on the problem and enables you to build intimacy. Good communication incorporates some basic principles such as recognizing the 'emotional you' beneath the physical and material needs, active listening, and making feedback both acceptable and effective. Active listening is actually wanting to really listen to what is in the other person's heart and mind. I want to be understanding of the other person's position. I communicate I am listening and understanding in the empathizer role. You use your normal empathy in relationships to be a good sounding board and active listener to help your partner work through their issues. The empathizer functions on the side of the sir's behavior of a helpful partner who supports her man.

CHAPTER 9

Embracing Feminine Qualities in Leadership

Neither Effren nor the editors of Psyche were suggesting that Yin, femininity, and masculinity, or such qualities as aggression or empathy, are inherent to either gender or linked to the sexual apparatus. Supposedly masculine people are thin on the ground and most of the males I know exhibit many supposedly feminine qualities. The 'fair sex', as Oscar Wilde observed, is anything but fair – it is well-nigh impossible to argue with. And, as anyone who has been in psychoanalysis will assure you, men are every bit as fractious, changeable, and irrational as women. As psychoanalysis reveals, none of us live up to our gender stereotypes if we know what is good for us.

Also, in this discussion of Yin and Yang, let's not lose sight of the contribution of the nurturing father. I do not think that Agland and Safina quite claim that a brief exposure – 50,000 years – to fatherly care was responsible for nurturing our empathy. But it would be well if we did not neglect a force that has such power to change our hormonal balance and soften our heart. Which is why it is so good to find that CEOs who come out as gay or as women come out in favor of 'diversity' – meaning that women are no worse than men and that not all women are socialist nitwits. There is small evidence that they are listening to the siren sounds of Yin but it is a start and have faith on faith we will build.

Empathy in the Workplace

Empathy is primarily a feminine energy, and a lot of this talk is an advertisement for embracing feminine energy. We are moving into ages where men also need to function in the feminine energy role, to tune into empathy, to stop always reacting to issues and 'fix' it, just to listen. We need men who can also do that, which is not so usual in society. For this reason, a lot of the company managers now, for the lowest levels of management, are women, as it just helps to manage the workplace and the employees, having more people that can listen and understand the problems of those working around them. I have been manipulated, watched colleagues lose their jobs, feeling and seeing what it has done to work morale, being scared for their futures and I cannot help but cast my mind outside our office – towards all the others going through the same thing just out there. You become more honest in the way you treat people with more empathy.

I support good company energies – supportive energies which accept all for who and what they are, and inclusive energies that allow people to enter into the workplace in peace. As I see it, moving into ages where real humanity, of all colors and creeds, is supported is an objective for the future of the world, and all these energies can work in with such a vision. Emphasizing the feminine capacity for empathy that is floundering at times – to the point where we should place emphasis on accepting people – would also transform our ideas of leadership. Leaders may not always be the ones who shout the most slogans or bark about the battleground. We may be able to begin to appreciate that leaders should be those that feel for their fellows and wish to rise higher together. In the future, the child, adult, or department that is being empathized with for going through a difficult workplace, be it real or imagined, or the trouble of working in a large company, needs to strive for personal and community solutions as well.

CHAPTER 10

Nurturing Self-Care and Well-Being

Delve into nurturing self-care - "me time" - a way of releasing stress while opening your heart and your spirit. The following practices open up the more receptive, softer NF places within us: massage, facials, journaling, meditation, restorative yoga, walking, options, soaking in a cold ocean, sitting near a pond or bay, taking time out of every day to do whatever non-work exercise activity will free the warrior woman and give permission to the more receptive, smaller one to play. Gentle weeding, stroking the dog, playing fetch, talking with friends over tea, or in person.

Integral to the healing and the acceptance of the feminine are the integration of self-care practices and the study and teaching of stress management. Because this world dominates, many women are caught in their own suffering or the denial of the pain of the world leaves them in an often hard-edged and therefore not very integrated, once again denying place. Women are poorly functioning, well at least in part, because they resist the transformational process; they are afraid of what might be transformed. They have seen bad transformations, the dramatic women's lettered playing Carly Simon's "give up" on the piano in the background. For women who have too many men to fully participate in our programs, we self-reducing defense armor part before they take the risk to come out from behind old invitations and out-find low energy, then we'll get some men everyone which we give them a forum in a hall, a type of group or in a program, we often say "heaven is calm". We can focus on women because women so often are the opposite part of the spiritual-cultural God role of this evolution caregiving and nurturing and being receptive, that all of the things that a lot of men that we do, sometimes as the subtext are communicated in her discussion and teaching equally a devoted mother will evoke, all this are dark values. Whether bringing into the transformation of the devotion of the start, not only said that they were not well time for personal transformation, anyone could say there was a time in the last too many men have come to say that well at least I'm just in this to be a better lover and have more sex with women which means the model and be softer to my children, don't beat the dogs, and pat me when I'm a little flipped out.

Mindfulness and Stress Management
Mindfulness and Stress Management: The practice of mindfulness has become more popular in recent years. Its influence is something that is greatly beneficial to nurturing self-care and well-being. Mindfulness lets us become less reactive and more accepting. It offers a form of stress management that allows people to build more emotional intelligence. Rather than simply addressing what causes stress for only partial relief, we encourage mastering good stress management via building emotional intelligence. When we recover from overload and learn good stress management, the practice naturally allows for personal transformation to occur. Because of that, opportunities to embrace feminine energy become more apparent. For this reason, and numerous others, we encourage practice and the devel-

opment of emotional intelligence. Various practices and techniques can be used for this purpose. Typically one refers to mindfulness when using the techniques for managing stress.

Embracing Feminine Energy: My personal preference in nurturing self-care and mindfulness is mindfulness and yoga, which is excellent for stress management. For the purpose of this teaching, one does not need any specific practice preference. We encourage people to bring more mindfulness into activities in their daily life so that they might embrace the feminine aspects more fully. Notice, mindfulness refers to being fully present to whatever one is doing, no matter how mundane or repetitious. This is a key to the practice of mindfulness. Further, choosing at least one specific activity in which to nurture the focus of the mind to single-pointed attention can itself build a sense of the feminine.

CHAPTER 11

The Role of Feminine Energy in Romantic Relationsh

Directing feminine energy into romantic love, or other forms of it, has also considerably different purposes and ways to be expressed than that when the object of love is the whole world. Loving a person and expressing all the beauty and grace of being genuinely feminine to create a connection isn't quite the same as being your feminine self in the face of a beautiful landscape at sunset, or the sun, moon, or stars at night. The same, indeed, can relate to business relationships, traditional gender norms, and many other ways feminine energy can be expressed cross-culturally.

Feminine energy is a quality as well as a relationship of "flow" that, above all else, is revealingly different than the traditional definitions of rationalistic science, maleness, and/or what is traditionally conceived of as "the light" in the New Age and personal growth movements. Once masculine and feminine begin emerging beyond the customary limits of a particular individual, creativity and change for breaking the cycle of discord and building more satisfying relationships emerge. Often, it is identified that, in doing personal development, spiritual and psychological healing and forgiveness, and learning how to love, the coasting mechanism underlying these feminine "values" can bring men across loud and clear. In addition, although perhaps not as much as it may take with women, very frequently when men embrace these feminine energetic qualities, they re-surprise their female lover with more love, passion, and serenity.

Creating Intimacy and Connection

Why open to embracing this side? When we do, it becomes infinitely easier to create connection and intimacy in the context of a romantic relationship. At first, this embraces the idea that most good qualities live within the feminine. Now, on an essential level, we all possess both qualities. Men possess incredible depth, sensitivity, and nurturing. Relationships struggling or lacking these essential core elements irrevocably harm men. Men who turn away from these qualities suffer. On a deeper level, to deny them denies the very meaning of femininity itself. Take this from a woman who struggled mightily with these issues in my own life, who was wound so tightly refused to open up to anyone: I was being a really crappy woman! I wore my perfection like Victoria wears a bra: define yourself with it and protect your heart with a wall of steel and padding.

Since embracing and integrating my feminine energy, I've attracted some of the most beautiful men on the planet - they know how to make us women smile! The reason for it speaks to a very important truth: we stand to learn and embrace tools which transform us into the kind of men women love to date. It all begins with your willingness to open and flower your own emotions. On a basic primal level, the woman's body was created to intimately birth life. Energy freely circulating within you furthers this. This isn't to say you must let the world in and emotionally expose yourself on a second date.

CHAPTER 12

Harnessing Creativity and Passion

Tapping into our feminine energy allows us to embrace passion and creativity. Traditionally, masculine ways of thinking have been praised in society, but true creative expression relies more on the emotional depth of femininity. Creativity and passion depend on the very emotions that society has worked so hard to train us to suppress. Shift your energy toward the masculine, and you give up a significant amount of your capacity for artistic expression. This is a bit of a disaster for both your life and your relationships. Passionate expression can be a catalyst that transforms you into a more vibrant, present, and alive man.

Great paintings display a stunning beauty and depth and vibrancy that comes only through the contrast and balance of the various colors in the painting. In much the same way, people who have embraced both their masculine and feminine energies boast an intangible, passionate something that draws people to them like moths to a flame. Whether artist or businessperson, being truly wild and yet also in control can make you a success. When you let go of society's need to differentiate and just be yourself, you convey the image of someone who is genuinely creative and open to new ideas. You come across as a risk-taker who isn't afraid to improvise solutions. When you live in definitive acceptance of both aspects of yourself, people will sense the safety and reliability that radiates off of you. This ability to deal with the unknown attracts others to you, like moths to a flame. These are the people in business, in love, in relationships, and in life who go the distance.

Expressing Emotions through Art

Effectively positioning oneself within the realms of vulnerability requires an honest and authentic openness. While many people may consider themselves emotionally naive, the reality of expressing deep, innermost emotions is wholly socialized away. This may cause a logjam of unsentimentality; as such, many may realize that their preferred means of emotional expression is sublimation. Art—whether it be to create literature, film, painting, or another form—might serve as an evocative means to widen that emotional stream.

Embracing Feminine Energy

It is well known that in astrology, the symbol for the feminine principle—the Moon—is similarly tied to the emotions, intuition, and instinct. Our Western allegories of "Mother Soul" reflect these associations of depths and feeling. While the specificities of these symbols and their meanings do not directly reflect the individual, utilizing various outlets as a means for emotional depth and intuition has some merit. It is important to one's growth that they may transform themselves into something more than what they currently are. As a result of this ongoing struggle toward reformation – to become something more profound and honest—it is beneficial to embrace feminine energy. In essence, such energy encourages a pursuit toward the expression of something more deeply personal and emotive, rather than detached and logical.

In other words, by integrating the masculinity of our being with a feminine element, we might facilitate effective connective work; in doing so, we express a more profoundly earnest side of ourselves. By expressing our emotions and incorporating our highest self into our identity, we rebuild the inconsistencies and become more aligned with love and passion. We can find evidence for the transformative power of feminine energy (that is, apart from its accommodating symbols – the emotions and intuition) through mediums that embrace vulnerability and explore femininity as a facet of their appeal.

CHAPTER 13

Spiritual Growth and Inner Transformation

Embracing feminine energy goes beyond the physical, emotional, and mental planes of personal evolution. It is one aspect of spiritual growth that each of us can contribute to with our inner transformation. Inner transformation can only happen if we have enough spiritual energy. Our accumulated spiritual power allows the physical transformation to happen, where testosterone changes the balance of our essence. So, we need to combine these transformations (personal, spiritual, physical/essence) as the main goal for the transformation of men toward a different kind of man who uses more spiritual energy to manifest their essential selves.

Everybody needs to embrace more and more their feminine energies for real transformation. It is not only up to men, nor is the transformation of men loosely related to the personal or spiritual growth of any individual. It is interrelated. That is why we are building spiritual groups for the well-being and freedom of the participants. Confronting and embracing the essence means a different kind of connection between men, to finally connect men and women (that will be written in the next few years). It also means a different way to relate to our groups and the world. Our groups can have a light of their own that creates an environment that allows the very deep spiritual growth to unfold. That is the most spiritual environment we have in Oshana groups, where all energy goes into spirituality; love and passion are equal in our groups and there is no energy outside the spiritual path.

Connecting with Higher Consciousness

To experience the wisdom of the divine feminine – men turn to higher consciousness.

The quickest way to come into the divine feminine that is within you in your heart is then to read scripture. This will move you that much more into a higher realm of consciousness where all transactions are in love. And men will feel the passion within their hearts because it is so transcendent that it is beyond passion in the lower forms. Deep down, a burning love for the spoken word will blossom within. This is the touch of the feminine. This is the truth within.

The knowledge of the scripture turns one into the silence of the heart, untold excitement and joy beyond expression arises. Women, even though they need the wisdom of the scriptures to really understand themselves in this moment of history, are already at the stage of love and passion and all they need to do is to integrate these two and all of life. Deepest silence in the mind and loving compassionate eye contact. Beyond all, the ultimate understanding of the essence of love and passion is through the realization of who I am – that non-dual consciousness – vibrant energy that sustains the creation. While here, it is good that we apply some of the principles learned. Attend to life in a way that you know is possible: love the male and awaken the female. Consciously create life and treat him like your own and receive all that you deserve. From the heart. Consciously. Embracing the female.

CHAPTER 14

Embracing Diversity and Inclusivity

We should be proud of our diversity and inclusivity. It's what sets us apart from algorithms that prescribe content that someone else has decided we should see. It's what makes our community vibrant and gives us opportunities to learn about different perspectives and to embrace the beauty that every individual brings to love and partnership.

As you will see, pursuing a love of emotions can lead to a metamorphosis in and of itself. A beautiful love. Ladies, your bond with one another is not only to support each other, but to share what's on the other side of this transformation. If we can unite, beyond race, religion, and sexuality, and see each other's point of view and respect it, we can unite men in the same way. We can collectively share what we have learned, the need for this kind of love, what we want from it, how to get it, and the extraordinary passion it can bring. We can choose to be, and are becoming, women who respect everyone in their individual journeys of femininity and diversity. To be proud of others' journeys, rather than threatened by it. Think of being part of the paradigm shift back to the 'way things used to be,' the good way things used to be, before things got twisted—the fairytales, or the polarity of mythical beasts and warriors, modern-day gods of thunder and magic, and warrior princesses. Expensive corporate dresses and jeans just won't do. It's the dressing up for a love and passion worth having.

Respecting Different Perspectives

When I wrote this book, I was taught not to use my own truths, so I might be missing something. I will always have a point of view, a lived experience, a stereograph, a divine perspective if you will, for embracing feminine energy. This perspective will change everything; it will include everything. That divine perspective is also a human one. The Buddhist author and living Buddha, Thich Nhat Hanh, encourages the mindful exploration of human suffering through the practice of deep listening. As I wrote, I opened my heart and I listened to everyone who resided in it.

Embracing feminine energy can only happen part of the time for many people who wish for a romantic outcome. The confusion is totally understandable. Many could not embrace their own feminine energy; we could not reap the rewards of such an understanding until we learned to live inside of it. I also wanted to respect those who may disagree. It is liberating to live in a time for human beings where true love and passion live in so many different kinds of relationships. Too real for me and for many to imagine; I had to let everyone in; in respect for the existence of so many different perspectives, I had to let go, a little, of my own. Maybe just in my mind, if not in my heart. If A New Dawn can exist in so many hearts, then the peace that emanates from it will travel into a new world that must always be transformed by diversity and inclusivity. If it doesn't, we can again transform love and passion the way we always have: exactly as we imagined it.

CHAPTER 15

The Evolution of Masculinity in Modern Society

As women seek to define themselves as more than just bodies, men need a new paradigm of relating to those bodies. As the rise of the feminine permeates business, politics, and society, these lone figures on the cliffs need to "evolve or die" as they themselves might say. Women have transformed themselves. What is the new way of being to which we wish to be loved?

The Evolution of Masculinity in Modern Society: Part of the New Masculinity Movement and its perspectives on masculinity, gender, and love is born of crucial shifts in the social and gender landscape. The psychologists John Moore, Sam Keen, and Robert Bly, influential figures in the new movement, all of whom addressed the public in conferences recorded in the late 1980s and early 1990s, talk about "tearing down the old system of power". Gay Hendricks denounces men at once "emotionally castrated" (powerful, cold, technical) and "psychologically castrated" (needy, weak, womanish, passive). Despite their differences, these psychologists locate within the culture an enduring ideal of rugged (not rich) individualism, emotional suppression accompanied by the harnessing of women to fulfill distinct, gender-specific roles. Moore and Keen pivot into spirituality, Greco-Roman mythologies, and the essential "energy" of masculinity, which is separate and denied by modern America, even ironically by New Age movements that lay capacity for the sacred entirely in the woman. In the landscape painted by both tendentious discourses, women are revealed (in the best-case scenario) as mature, complete—grown other than men.

The remainder of this section is written with the understanding that such perspectives do not reflect the experiences of every person, that generalizations about a "mainstream culture" exist to be analyzed, disassembled, and that none are served by blanket prescriptions governed by gender-normativity. The critiques informed by Moore, Keen, and Bly's prescription as well as popular literature on men's health are several. My primary contentions are that the "old" Hokmi bloke—parent of Little Women and Little Men alike—is no more representative of masculinity than Tom Breeze is an accurate picture of the rise of a physically-sick, morally-decayed "Weariness" in early American literature. I believe masculinity is in a state of change but point out that change has always been the case, patterns notwithstanding. Finally, in the subsequent pages, I want to operationalize what "masculine" looks like to me, using identification not to exclude femininity but to create a historical record to which a heterogeneous experience of masculine can lay formal claim. Inquilinizing taste might pop up anywhere in the cultural products of rural America. Descriptions of masculinity entertained herein are not timeless but reflect my analysis of popular images and conceptions of "men" as distinct from "humans" at different moments in American culture. I transform the supposedly feminine category of popular "Chick Flicks" paradigmatic in film criticism into a site for reconsidering the tentatively opposing sign of "Bromances," positioning paternal melodrama as model masculinity and fulfillment. I have done so, however, only by demonstrating the deeply-embedded femininity of the tears in little boys, adopting a truer humanist perspective of love ungendered, if possible at all.

Shifting Paradigms

Something is transforming in the very core of masculinity today. We can sense this shift in our silence, in our restlessness, dissatisfactions, greatness, longings, sorrows, and love. In the recent past, the very idea of masculinity was seen as a certain rigid behavior, certain attitudes, beliefs, and understanding demonstrated by a person who had come of age. At the core of this definition is the concept of 'power,' of being all-powerful, and an absolute ruler. On the contrary, today we see, we live the reality of the possibility of a man as a lover.

Our understanding of what being biologically masculine implies is also changing. Across the religions, societies throughout the world, existing masculinity has drawn up the roles on the basis of which they treat their women, in thought and action. However, in practice, there is a peace movement and the basic shift happening among the good old masculine fraternity. The stigma of not being a man, or enough of a man, or being any less of a woman is a double wound. As we have seen in the preceding chapters, not only does it bruise the one it is directed towards; it hurts the one who disciplines and redirects and oppresses for fear of inadequacy. Moreover, as it has been said, error need not be all bad. Where else will life find the lessons? Our collective humanity is on the brink of an initiation into The New Convention where the ability to forge alliances, take risks, make commitments, and the discipline to believe and work for their commitments instead of division is a sought wealth. The definitions of what is 'masculine' and what is 'feminine' are expanding.

CHAPTER 16

Conclusion: Embracing Feminine Energy for Personal

The journey has been transformative. For many of you reading my words, you have accepted parts of yourself you were originally not very happy about. You've started pleasing yourself for a change and acting on your own behalf instead of waiting for the world to change around you. And even when that journey has taken you through hike after hike into the loneliness in your being, you have come out the other side every single time. It has left its scars, but it has brushed and polished your soul too, and oh, how it shines. Even when you are shivering from the aftershock, you are all fired up about the fact that the world will never be the same again.

That is the beauty of it. Really, it is. It has created a spark that has set other fires about. Furthermore, energy works on a quantum level: your embrace of your feminine energy travels through time and space. It embraces you, and you embrace her and we all embrace each other at the same time. It is in the line of self-love instead of self-sacrifice, and it is in there that we grow our capacity to embrace many more, collectively. It is also something one has to actually live and apply to know what I mean. As much as I've written here about solving issues in your relationships or between you and the masculine force in the world, the real invitation here is one to let us all transform, as a result of embracing energy that has been simply transformative. Can you imagine a society in which every single woman truly stands for her love and her passion? How society would have to re-align itself to become truly for all women?

www.ingramcontent.com/pod-product-compliance
Lightning Source LLC
Chambersburg PA
CBHW051500140726
47987CB00006B/2812